25 REASONS WHY PEOPLE FAIL IN BUSINESS

ASSURED PATHWAYS TO PROSPERITY FOR COMPANIES, ENTREPRENEURS AND BUSINESS OWNERS

BY

ELION BUFFET

Starting and running a business is a challenging endeavor that demands dedication, strategic thinking, and adaptability. Despite the best intentions, many entrepreneurs find themselves facing setbacks that lead to failure. In this book, we explore some of the key reasons why people fail in business.

Failure in business can result from a variety of factors. Here are 25 vital reasons why people may fail in business that established and prospective entrepreneurs must know:

1

LACK OF CLEAR BUSINESS PLAN

Lack of a Clear Business Plan Can Spell Failure in the fast-paced and competitive world of business, having a clear roadmap is crucial for success. However, some entrepreneurs underestimate the importance of a well-defined business plan, putting their ventures at risk of failure. Here's a closer look at how the absence of a clear business plan can be a recipe for disaster.

Directionless Decision-Making:
Without a solid business plan, entrepreneurs may find themselves navigating their ventures without a clear sense of direction. This lack of guidance can lead to haphazard decision-making, increasing the likelihood of making choices that are not aligned with the overall goals and vision of the business.

Inadequate Resource Management:
A detailed business plan helps in outlining the necessary resources for the venture. Without this guidance, businesses may struggle with resource allocation, leading to inefficiencies and financial strain. Poor

resource management can impede growth and hinder the ability to capitalize on opportunities.

Unrealistic Expectations:
A well-crafted business plan includes realistic financial projections and goals. Without such a plan, entrepreneurs may set unattainable expectations, both for themselves and their stakeholders. This can result in disappointment, eroding confidence, and support from investors, partners, and employees.

Limited Investor Appeal:
Investors often look for a clear and comprehensive business plan before committing their funds. Without a compelling roadmap, entrepreneurs may struggle to attract investors, limiting their access to crucial capital for growth and development.

Ineffective Marketing Strategies:
Marketing efforts should be aligned with business objectives. Without a plan, businesses may engage in inconsistent or ineffective marketing strategies, failing to reach their target audience and build a strong brand presence in the market.

Risk of Overlooking Contingencies:
Business plans are essential for identifying potential risks and devising strategies to mitigate them. The absence of a plan leaves businesses vulnerable to unforeseen challenges, such as economic downturns or industry shifts, with no contingency measures in place.

Employee Disengagement:
A clear business plan serves as a communication tool, conveying the company's mission and goals to employees. Without this guidance,

employees may feel disconnected from the overall purpose of the business, leading to decreased morale and productivity.

The lack of a clear business plan can have severe repercussions for a venture. Entrepreneurs must recognize that a well-thought-out business plan is not just a formality but a strategic necessity. It not only provides direction but also serves as a foundation for making informed decisions, attracting investors, and fostering sustainable growth. As the saying goes, failing to plan is planning to fail, and in the dynamic world of business, this sentiment holds truer than ever.

2

INSUFFICIENT MARKET RESEARCH

In the ever-evolving landscape of commerce, the role of thorough market research cannot be overstated. Entrepreneurs who underestimate the importance of understanding their market often find themselves on shaky ground, risking failure. Here's an exploration of how insufficient market research can be a critical factor in the downfall of businesses.

Mismatched Product-Market Fit:
Without comprehensive market research, businesses may launch products or services that do not resonate with the needs and preferences of their target audience. A lack of understanding of customer demands can lead to a significant disconnect between what is offered and what the market truly seeks.

Ineffective Marketing Strategies:

Market research is the foundation upon which effective marketing strategies are built. In its absence, businesses may struggle to identify their target demographics, resulting in misguided promotional efforts that fail to capture the attention of potential customers.

Unawareness of Competitors:
Understanding the competitive landscape is crucial for positioning a business effectively. Inadequate market research can leave entrepreneurs in the dark about competitors' strengths, weaknesses, and innovations, hindering their ability to differentiate and stay ahead in the market.

Pricing Pitfalls:
Pricing is a delicate balance that requires a deep understanding of market dynamics. Without thorough research, businesses may set prices either too high, deterring cost-conscious consumers, or too low, risking profitability. This lack of pricing precision can be detrimental to the bottom line.

Missed Opportunities:
Market research not only identifies existing market trends but also reveals emerging opportunities. Failing to invest in research means potentially overlooking lucrative niches or failing to capitalize on shifts in consumer behavior, putting the business at a disadvantage compared to more informed competitors.

Customer Dissatisfaction:
Insufficient knowledge of customer expectations can result in subpar products or services. This, in turn, leads to dissatisfied customers, negative reviews, and a tarnished reputation. In today's interconnected world, a single dissatisfied customer can have a ripple effect on the brand's image.

Risk of Overexpansion or Contraction:
Market research is crucial for strategic decision-making regarding business expansion or contraction. Without a clear understanding of market demand and trends, businesses may make misguided decisions, risking overexpansion into saturated markets or premature contraction in areas with growth potential.

Inability to Anticipate Industry Shifts:
Industries are dynamic, with trends and technologies evolving rapidly. Insufficient market research leaves businesses vulnerable to unexpected industry shifts, making it challenging to adapt and stay competitive in the long run.

The failure to conduct thorough market research is akin to navigating a complex maze blindfolded. Businesses must recognize that understanding the market is not just a one-time activity but an ongoing process crucial for informed decision-making and sustainable growth. In a world where consumer preferences and market dynamics are in constant flux, businesses that invest in comprehensive market research are better equipped to navigate challenges and thrive in the competitive arena.

3

POOR FINANCIAL MANAGEMENT

In the intricate dance of business, financial management takes center stage as a critical determinant of success. Entrepreneurs who neglect this aspect of their ventures often find themselves on a perilous path, risking failure. Here's an examination of how poor financial management can be a decisive factor in the downfall of businesses.

Cash Flow Crunch:
Poor financial management often leads to inadequate cash flow, leaving businesses struggling to meet day-to-day expenses. Without a firm grip on cash flow, even profitable ventures can face liquidity crises, hindering their ability to seize opportunities or weather economic downturns.

Excessive Debt Burden:
Failure to manage debt effectively can result in an overwhelming burden that stifles business growth. Poor financial planning may lead to taking on excessive loans or lines of credit without a clear repayment strategy, leading to mounting interest payments and a potential debt spiral.

Inaccurate Budgeting:
A well-crafted budget is the cornerstone of financial stability. In the absence of accurate budgeting, businesses may find themselves overspending or allocating resources inefficiently, undermining their ability to allocate funds to critical areas such as marketing, research, and development.

Lack of Financial Resilience:
Businesses with poor financial management are ill-equipped to withstand unforeseen challenges. Whether it's a sudden market shift, a global crisis, or industry-specific disruptions, a lack of financial resilience leaves businesses vulnerable to external shocks that can be insurmountable without a financial safety net.

Inefficient Resource Allocation:

Poor financial management often leads to suboptimal resource allocation. This can result in underinvestment in areas crucial for growth, such as technology upgrades, employee training, or market research. Inefficient resource allocation impedes a business's ability to stay competitive and innovate.

Employee Dissatisfaction and Turnover:
Financial instability can impact payroll reliability and employee benefits. This, in turn, can lead to dissatisfaction among employees, affecting morale and productivity. High turnover rates due to financial uncertainties can disrupt operations and increase recruitment costs.

Lack of Strategic Investments:
Businesses need to make strategic investments to stay relevant and competitive. Poor financial management may prevent ventures from seizing opportunities for expansion, innovation, or market penetration, limiting their ability to evolve and thrive in dynamic industries.

Uninformed Decision-Making:
Financial data is crucial for informed decision-making. Without accurate financial information, businesses may make decisions based on assumptions rather than concrete evidence. This can lead to misguided strategies and a lack of agility in responding to market changes.

Without any doubt, poor financial management is akin to navigating a storm without a compass. Entrepreneurs must recognize that financial health is not a byproduct but a strategic imperative for business survival. By implementing sound financial practices, businesses can build resilience, foster growth, and position themselves for long-term success in the unpredictable landscape of commerce.

4

INADEQUATE FUNDING OR CAPITAL

In the intricate tapestry of entrepreneurship, securing adequate funding is often the linchpin that determines a business's success or failure. Entrepreneurs who underestimate the importance of robust capitalization may find their ventures teetering on the brink. Here's a voyage of how inadequate funding can be a decisive factor in the downfall of businesses.

Stunted Growth Opportunities:
Inadequate funding limits a business's ability to capitalize on growth opportunities. Whether it's expanding operations, entering new markets, or investing in research and development, a shortage of funds restrains a business from reaching its full potential and staying competitive in dynamic industries.

Insufficient Marketing Reach:
Marketing is crucial for brand visibility and customer acquisition. However, without sufficient capital, businesses may struggle to implement effective marketing strategies, limiting their reach and hindering the ability to connect with target audiences. This can result in slower customer acquisition and market penetration.

Inability to Weather Economic Downturns:
Economic downturns are inevitable, and businesses need financial reserves to weather the storm. Inadequate funding leaves ventures vulnerable to external shocks, making it challenging to navigate

through economic recessions, industry downturns, or unexpected crises without facing severe financial strain.

Talent Acquisition Challenges:
Attracting and retaining top talent requires competitive salaries, benefits, and professional development opportunities. Insufficient funding hampers a business's ability to offer attractive compensation packages, leading to challenges in recruiting and retaining skilled employees critical for growth and innovation.

Lack of Innovation and Adaptability:
Innovation is the lifeblood of successful businesses. Inadequate funding stifles investment in research and development, limiting a business's ability to innovate and adapt to changing market trends. This lack of agility can result in becoming obsolete in a rapidly evolving business landscape.

Quality Compromises:
Producing high-quality products or services often requires significant investment. Inadequate funding may force businesses to cut corners, compromising on product or service quality. This not only jeopardizes customer satisfaction but also damages the brand's reputation in the long run.

Strained Relationships with Suppliers and Partners:
Late payments and strained cash flow due to insufficient funding can strain relationships with suppliers and business partners. This can lead to disruptions in the supply chain, increased costs, and, in extreme cases, legal complications that further hinder the business's financial stability.

Limited Risk Mitigation:

Every business faces risks, and having adequate funding is crucial for implementing risk mitigation strategies. Without a financial cushion, ventures may find it challenging to navigate unforeseen challenges, increasing the likelihood of business failure in the face of unexpected obstacles.

The inadequacy of funding is akin to attempting a cross-country journey with an empty gas tank. Entrepreneurs must recognize that securing ample capital is not just a financial consideration but a strategic necessity for navigating the unpredictable terrain of business. By prioritizing and securing sufficient funding, businesses can build resilience, pursue growth opportunities, and increase their chances of long-term success in the competitive world of entrepreneurship.

5

IGNORING CHANGING MARKET TRENDS

In the dynamic landscape of today's business world, ignoring changing market trends can be a perilous decision that leads to eventual failure. Businesses that fail to adapt and evolve with the ever-shifting market dynamics risk losing relevance, customer trust, and ultimately, their competitive edge.

Stagnation in Innovation:
Businesses that ignore market trends often become stagnant in their approach, relying on outdated products or services. This lack of innovation can result in a diminished appeal to consumers who are continually seeking the latest and most advanced solutions.

Loss of Customer Relevance:

Customers are the lifeblood of any business. Failing to recognize and respond to changing preferences and needs can lead to a loss of customer relevance. Consumers are drawn to businesses that understand and cater to their evolving expectations, and failure to do so can result in a decline in customer loyalty.

Increased Competition:
As market trends shift, new players emerge, and existing competitors adapt, the landscape becomes more competitive. Businesses that remain oblivious to these changes find themselves ill-equipped to compete effectively. Ignoring market trends allows competitors to gain a foothold, potentially leading to a loss of market share.

Technological Disruption:
Advancements in technology have a profound impact on market trends. Businesses that disregard technological shifts may find themselves blindsided by disruptive innovations, putting them at a significant disadvantage. Embracing technology and staying abreast of industry developments is crucial for long-term survival.

Economic Uncertainties:
Economic conditions are subject to change, and businesses must be adaptable to navigate fluctuations. Ignoring market trends, including economic indicators, can leave businesses vulnerable to unforeseen challenges. Those who fail to anticipate and respond to economic shifts may struggle to weather financial storms.

Evolving Consumer Behavior:
Consumer behavior is constantly evolving, influenced by societal changes, technological advancements, and cultural shifts. Businesses must stay attuned to these changes to effectively connect with their

target audience. Ignoring evolving consumer behavior can result in a disconnect between the business and its clientele.

Regulatory Compliance Challenges:
Market trends are not only influenced by consumer preferences but also by regulatory changes. Ignoring shifts in regulations can lead to non-compliance issues, legal challenges, and reputational damage. Businesses that stay informed and proactively adapt to regulatory changes demonstrate a commitment to ethical practices and long-term success.

The consequences of ignoring changing market trends are far-reaching and can spell disaster for businesses. To thrive in today's competitive environment, entrepreneurs and companies must embrace a culture of continuous adaptation, staying vigilant to shifts in consumer behavior, technology, and regulatory landscapes. By doing so, businesses can position themselves not only to survive but to flourish in the ever-changing marketplace.

6

WEAK OR INEXPERIENCED MANAGEMENT

In the dynamic landscape of business, the role of management is paramount. Weak or inexperienced management can act as a ticking time bomb, poised to detonate the success of any enterprise. Now, let's explore the critical ways in which inept management can lead a business down the path of failure.

Lack of Vision and Direction:

Ineffective management often struggles to articulate a clear vision for the company. Without a compelling direction, employees may become disengaged and lose sight of the organization's goals. A cohesive vision is the compass that guides a business through challenges and uncertainties.

Poor Decision-Making:
Inexperienced managers may lack the acumen needed to make strategic decisions. Whether it's financial choices, market positioning, or resource allocation, weak management can make ill-informed decisions that jeopardize the company's stability and growth.

Employee Morale and Productivity:
A disengaged or inept management team can create a toxic work environment. Low morale among employees can lead to decreased productivity, increased turnover, and a decline in overall organizational performance. A motivated workforce is a cornerstone of business success.

Ineffective Communication:
Clear communication is the lifeblood of any successful organization. Weak management often fails to communicate effectively, leading to misunderstandings, misalignment of objectives, and a breakdown in teamwork. This lack of communication can ripple through the entire company, causing operational inefficiencies.

Ignoring Talent Development:
Competent management understands the importance of nurturing talent within the organization. Inexperienced leaders may neglect employee development, hindering the growth of the workforce and leaving the company ill-prepared to face industry challenges.

Failure to Adapt to Change:
The business landscape is constantly evolving. Weak management may resist change or fail to adapt to new market trends and technologies. This rigidity can result in the company becoming obsolete or losing its competitive edge.

Financial Mismanagement:
Financial acumen is a crucial skill for effective management. Inexperienced leaders may mishandle budgets, fail to control costs, or make poor investment decisions. Financial instability can quickly snowball into a full-blown crisis for the business.

In a nutshell, the consequences of weak or inexperienced management are far-reaching and can spell disaster for a business. To thrive in the competitive business world, organizations must invest in developing strong, capable leaders who can navigate challenges, inspire their teams, and steer the company toward sustainable success. The price of neglecting the importance of robust management is too high, and the repercussions can be felt across every facet of the business.

7

OVEREXPANSION TOO QUICKLY

In the pursuit of success, businesses often face the tempting prospect of expansion. However, the adage "too much, too soon" holds true, especially when it comes to rapid overexpansion. This section delves into the pitfalls that businesses can encounter when they expand hastily, exploring the potential causes of failure in the wake of such decisions.

Strained Resources:
One of the immediate consequences of overexpansion is the strain on resources. Scaling up operations too quickly can lead to a shortage of capital, manpower, and infrastructure. Insufficient resources can hinder day-to-day operations, compromise product or service quality, and ultimately erode customer satisfaction.

Operational Inefficiencies:
Expansion often requires adjustments to existing processes and systems. Rapid growth can outpace an organization's ability to adapt, resulting in operational inefficiencies. This can lead to bottlenecks, communication breakdowns, and a general loss of control over the business's core functions.

Market Saturation:
Expanding into new markets without proper analysis can result in oversaturation. Overestimating demand or underestimating competition can lead to a scenario where the market cannot support the increased supply. This oversaturation can dilute brand value and diminish the business's overall market position.

Deteriorating Quality Control:
Maintaining consistent product or service quality becomes increasingly challenging during rapid expansion. Businesses may struggle to uphold the standards that initially garnered success, leading to customer dissatisfaction and, ultimately, a decline in reputation.

Financial Strain:
Overexpansion often demands significant financial investment. If not carefully managed, this can lead to financial strain and debt accumulation. Businesses may find themselves in a precarious

financial position, unable to meet obligations or invest in crucial areas such as innovation and marketing.

Cultural Dilution:
As companies expand, maintaining a cohesive organizational culture becomes challenging. The core values that once defined the business can get diluted across geographies or departments, leading to a loss of identity and unity among employees.

Lack of Market Understanding:
Expanding into new territories without a thorough understanding of local markets can result in misguided strategies. Different regions may have unique consumer behaviors, regulatory environments, and cultural nuances that demand careful consideration. Ignoring these factors can lead to misalignment with the target audience.

Inability to Adapt:
The business environment is dynamic, and overexpansion can make it difficult for an organization to adapt swiftly to changes. Rigidity in the face of market shifts, technological advancements, or economic downturns can leave a business vulnerable to failure.

While expansion is a natural part of business growth, the key lies in measured and strategic moves. Overexpansion without proper planning and consideration of potential risks can lead to a cascade of challenges, ultimately culminating in failure. Success in business demands a delicate balance between ambition and prudence, ensuring that growth is sustainable, controlled, and aligned with the organization's capabilities and market realities.

8

<u>INEFFECTIVE MARKETING AND BRANDING</u>

In the fast-paced world of commerce, where first impressions matter more than ever, the significance of effective marketing and branding cannot be overstated. This section of the book delves into the critical role these elements play in determining the success or failure of a business, exploring the repercussions of ineffective strategies in these key areas.

Lost in the Crowd:
In a market saturated with choices, businesses must stand out to capture consumer attention. Ineffective marketing fails to differentiate a brand from its competitors, rendering it indistinguishable in the eyes of potential customers. This lack of distinctiveness can lead to obscurity and, ultimately, failure.

Misaligned Messaging:
A coherent and compelling brand message is the backbone of successful marketing. When messaging is unclear, inconsistent, or fails to resonate with the target audience, businesses risk alienating potential customers. Misaligned messaging can confuse consumers about a brand's identity and values, eroding trust and loyalty.

Poor Visibility:
Even the most revolutionary products or services can flounder without proper visibility. Ineffective marketing strategies may result in a lack of exposure, leaving businesses struggling to reach their target audience. Limited visibility hampers growth and can stifle a company's potential to expand its market share.

Failure to Establish Emotional Connections:

Successful branding goes beyond logos and slogans; it establishes an emotional connection with consumers. When branding lacks authenticity or fails to evoke the desired sentiments, businesses miss an opportunity to create lasting relationships with their audience. Emotional connections are the bedrock of brand loyalty.

Wasted Resources:
Ineffective marketing can lead to the inefficient allocation of resources. Businesses may invest in channels or tactics that do not resonate with their audience, resulting in a waste of time and budget. Misguided efforts can drain financial resources without delivering the expected return on investment.

Reputation Damage:
A poorly executed marketing campaign or inconsistent branding can tarnish a company's reputation. Negative perceptions, once established, are challenging to overcome. In the era of social media, where information travels swiftly, a damaged reputation can spell swift and severe consequences for a business.

Ignoring Digital Presence:
In today's digital age, a robust online presence is non-negotiable. Ineffective marketing often neglects the potential of digital platforms, missing out on a vast pool of potential customers. Ignoring the online landscape can leave businesses outpaced by more digitally savvy competitors.

Inability to Adapt to Market Trends:
Marketing is not a static endeavor; it evolves with consumer behaviors and market trends. Ineffective strategies often fail to adapt to changing landscapes, resulting in businesses falling behind the curve.

Stagnation in marketing approaches can leave a company obsolete in the eyes of its audience.

In the ever-evolving landscape of business, effective marketing and branding serve as linchpins for success. Businesses must recognize the profound impact these elements have on shaping perceptions, building relationships, and driving growth. By investing in thoughtful, strategic approaches to marketing and branding, businesses can navigate the competitive terrain and avoid the pitfalls that come with ineffectiveness in these crucial areas.

9

IGNORING CUSTOMER FEEDBACK

In the digital age, where connectivity and communication thrive, customer feedback stands as a powerful compass guiding businesses toward success. Ignoring this valuable input can have severe consequences, ranging from diminished customer satisfaction to outright business failure. Now, let's explore the critical importance of heeding customer feedback and the perils that come with neglecting this essential aspect of customer relations.

Disconnect from Customer Needs:
Customer feedback serves as a direct line to understanding their needs and expectations. Ignoring feedback creates a dangerous disconnect, leaving businesses unaware of evolving customer preferences. This ignorance can lead to a mismatch between the products or services offered and what the market demands, ultimately resulting in a decline in customer satisfaction and loyalty.

Quality Erosion:
Customers often provide insights into the quality of products or services. Ignoring their feedback can lead to a gradual erosion of quality standards. Without a vigilant approach to customer concerns, businesses risk delivering subpar experiences, damaging their reputation, and eroding trust in the brand.

Missed Innovation Opportunities:
Customers are a wellspring of ideas and suggestions for improvement. Dismissing their feedback means missing out on valuable insights that could drive innovation. Businesses that fail to embrace customer-driven innovation may find themselves lagging behind competitors who leverage this feedback to enhance their offerings.

Negative Word-of-Mouth:
Unaddressed customer issues can escalate, leading to negative word-of-mouth. In the era of social media and online reviews, disgruntled customers have powerful platforms to share their experiences. Ignoring feedback amplifies the likelihood of negative publicity, tarnishing the brand's image and deterring potential customers.

Eroded Customer Trust:
Trust is a fragile commodity in business, and customer feedback plays a pivotal role in maintaining it. Ignoring feedback signals to customers that their opinions are undervalued, eroding trust in the brand. Businesses that dismiss customer concerns risk losing the foundation upon which strong, enduring customer relationships are built.

Inability to Adapt to Market Changes:
Market dynamics are in constant flux, and customer feedback provides invaluable insights into emerging trends and shifts in

preferences. Ignoring this feedback leaves businesses vulnerable to being blindsided by market changes. The inability to adapt can lead to obsolescence and eventual failure in the face of more agile competitors.

Unresolved Issues Piling Up:
Customer feedback often highlights recurring issues or pain points. Ignoring these persistent problems allows them to accumulate, creating a snowball effect that can overwhelm a business. Unresolved issues can lead to customer frustration, increased churn, and a damaged reputation that is challenging to repair.

Missed Opportunities for Improvement:
Every piece of feedback, positive or negative, is an opportunity for improvement. Ignoring this input denies businesses the chance to enhance their operations, refine their offerings, and elevate the overall customer experience. Over time, this stagnation can lead to a decline in competitiveness and relevance.

In the customer-centric landscape of modern business, the voice of the customer is an invaluable asset. Ignoring customer feedback is akin to navigating blindfolded, with the risk of stumbling into pitfalls that could have been avoided. Businesses that prioritize and actively listen to their customers not only build stronger relationships but also position themselves for sustainable growth in a competitive market. The cost of ignoring customer feedback is high, and the consequences can reverberate through every facet of a business, ultimately leading to failure.

10

INADEQUATE SALES AND REVENUE GENERATION

In the dynamic landscape of commerce, the heartbeat of any business lies in its ability to generate sales and revenue. When this fundamental aspect falters, it sets off a chain reaction that can lead to the eventual failure of the enterprise. In this section, we explore the profound implications of inadequate sales and revenue generation on businesses.

Financial Strain and Operational Hurdles:
Insufficient sales directly translate to a lack of revenue, putting immense strain on a company's financial health. This shortage of funds can impede day-to-day operations, hindering the ability to meet basic expenses such as payroll, utility bills, and procurement of essential resources. As financial strain escalates, it creates a domino effect that cripples a company's operational capabilities.

Inability to Invest in Innovation:
Thriving in the business world requires constant adaptation to market trends and technological advancements. Inadequate sales mean a lack of funds available for research and development. This hampers a company's ability to innovate and stay competitive, leaving it vulnerable to being overtaken by more agile and innovative competitors.

Erosion of Brand Image and Customer Trust:
Consistent sales are not only vital for financial stability but also for maintaining a positive brand image. A decline in sales may signal to customers and stakeholders that the business is struggling or losing relevance. This erosion of trust can be challenging to rebuild and may

result in a loss of customer loyalty, further exacerbating the sales downturn.

Reduced Marketing and Outreach Efforts:
Successful sales strategies often rely on effective marketing and outreach campaigns. When revenue is insufficient, businesses are forced to cut costs, and marketing budgets are often the first to suffer. This reduction in promotional efforts can lead to decreased brand visibility and diminished customer acquisition, perpetuating the cycle of inadequate sales.

Employee Morale and Productivity Decline:
A business in financial distress is likely to implement cost-cutting measures, which can include layoffs, salary reductions, or freezing hiring. This adversely affects employee morale and job satisfaction, leading to decreased productivity and innovation. A demoralized workforce further contributes to the challenges of turning around a business experiencing sales difficulties.

Debt Accumulation and Financial Dependency:
To cope with inadequate sales, businesses may resort to borrowing to meet their financial obligations. Accumulating debt, however, increases financial dependency and creates a burden that may become unsustainable over time. High debt levels not only strain the balance sheet but also limit the flexibility needed to navigate market fluctuations.

Inadequate sales and the subsequent revenue shortfall pose a multifaceted threat to businesses, affecting their financial stability, operational resilience, and long-term viability. Recognizing the warning signs early on and implementing strategic measures to boost sales is imperative for steering a company away from the precipice of failure. In the competitive landscape of modern commerce, adaptability, innovation, and a robust sales strategy are the cornerstones of sustained success.

11
IGNORING LEGAL AND REGULATORY REQUIREMENTS

In today's complex business landscape, adherence to legal and regulatory requirements is paramount for long-term success. Ignoring these crucial aspects can lead to severe consequences that may jeopardize the very foundation of a business.

Legal Repercussions:
Failure to comply with applicable laws can result in legal action, fines, or even business shutdowns. Regulatory bodies are tasked with ensuring businesses operate ethically and within the bounds of the law. Ignoring these requirements exposes companies to the risk of costly litigation and damage to their reputation.

Reputational Damage:
Public trust is a valuable asset in any business. Non-compliance tarnishes a company's reputation, eroding consumer trust and loyalty. In the age of social media and instant communication, negative news spreads quickly, affecting customer perception and stakeholder confidence.

Financial Implications:

Legal battles and regulatory fines incur significant financial costs. Ignoring compliance measures may lead to unforeseen expenditures that strain resources, impacting profitability and hindering the ability to invest in growth opportunities.

Operational Disruptions:
Regulatory requirements often dictate operational standards. Ignoring them may result in disruptions to daily business activities. Sudden closures, product recalls, or the halting of services can harm relationships with suppliers, customers, and partners.

International Business Challenges:
For companies operating globally, navigating diverse legal frameworks is crucial. Ignoring international legal and regulatory standards can result in barriers to entry, trade restrictions, and damaged relationships with foreign stakeholders.

Employee Morale and Retention:
Employees expect their employers to uphold ethical standards. Ignoring legal requirements may create a toxic work environment, leading to decreased morale and increased turnover. A disgruntled workforce can further damage a company's image.

Innovation and Adaptability:
Regulations are often designed to ensure fair competition and protect consumers. Ignoring them may hinder innovation and adaptability, as competitors who comply with regulations gain a competitive advantage. Long-term success requires a commitment to both legal and ethical business practices.

Businesses that overlook legal and regulatory requirements are playing a dangerous game. The consequences, ranging from legal troubles and financial losses to damaged reputations, can be severe. To thrive sustainably, companies must prioritize compliance, viewing it not only as a legal obligation but as a strategic imperative for long-term success.

12
FAILING TO ADAPT TO TECHNOLOGICAL ADVANCEMENTS

In the fast-paced world of business, adaptability is not just an advantage; it's a survival necessity. Failing to keep pace with technological advancements can set a company on a path toward irrelevance and ultimate failure.

Competitive Disadvantage:
Businesses that resist adopting new technologies risk falling behind competitors who leverage the latest tools for efficiency, productivity, and innovation. The modern marketplace rewards those who stay at the forefront of technological progress.

Inefficient Operations:
Outdated systems and processes hinder operational efficiency. Failing to embrace technological advancements can result in manual, time-consuming tasks that impede productivity and increase the likelihood of errors. Efficient operations are essential for maintaining a competitive edge.

Customer Expectations:
In the digital age, consumers expect seamless and convenient experiences. Businesses unable to adapt to evolving technological

trends risk alienating customers who seek modern, user-friendly interfaces, online services, and personalized interactions. Meeting and exceeding customer expectations is key to success.

Data Security Concerns:
As technology evolves, so do cybersecurity threats. Failing to invest in updated security measures can expose a business to data breaches, compromising customer trust and potentially leading to legal consequences. Protecting sensitive information is not just a best practice; it's a business imperative.

Innovation Stagnation:
Technological advancements often drive innovation. Companies resistant to adopting new technologies may find themselves unable to develop groundbreaking products or services, limiting their ability to stay relevant in dynamic markets.

Talent Attraction and Retention:
Top talent is drawn to organizations that embrace cutting-edge technologies. Failing to adapt may result in difficulties attracting skilled professionals, and existing employees may become disengaged if they feel their skills are stagnating. A tech-savvy workforce is a crucial asset for future growth.

Global Reach and Connectivity:
Technological advancements have made it easier for businesses to expand globally. Those reluctant to leverage digital tools may struggle to connect with international markets, missing out on opportunities for growth and diversification.

Cost of Catching Up:

Delaying technological adoption can create a backlog of necessary updates. The longer a business waits to embrace new technologies, the more costly and challenging it becomes to catch up. Proactive investment in technology is often more cost-effective than reactive measures.

The failure to adapt to technological advancements is a perilous choice for any business. In a landscape where change is constant, embracing innovation is not just a strategy—it's a survival instinct. Companies that prioritize staying ahead of the technological curve position themselves for sustained success in an ever-evolving business environment.

13

LACK OF A COMPETITIVE EDGE OR UNIQUE SELLING PROPOSITION

In the crowded marketplace of today, where consumers are inundated with choices, businesses must stand out to survive and thrive. A lack of a competitive edge or a unique selling proposition (USP) can leave a company vulnerable to failure.

Intense Market Competition:
Without a distinct competitive edge, businesses find themselves competing solely on price, leading to a race to the bottom. In a world saturated with options, consumers are drawn to companies that offer something unique, be it in product features, service quality, or overall experience.

Brand Differentiation:
A strong USP is the foundation of brand differentiation. Companies without a clear and compelling point of distinction may struggle to create a memorable brand identity. A unique selling proposition helps carve out a niche and fosters customer loyalty.

Customer Attraction and Retention:
Consumers are drawn to businesses that provide value beyond the ordinary. A lack of a competitive edge makes it challenging to attract new customers and retain existing ones. Offering something special or solving a unique problem creates a compelling reason for customers to choose one brand over another.

Adaptability to Market Changes:
In a rapidly evolving business environment, a unique selling proposition allows a company to adapt more easily to market changes. Businesses with a clear differentiator can adjust their strategies while maintaining a consistent brand identity, ensuring relevance in changing circumstances.

Pricing Strategy Challenges:
Without a competitive edge, businesses often resort to price competition, which can lead to reduced profit margins and financial instability. A unique selling proposition enables companies to justify premium pricing by offering value that goes beyond cost considerations.

Innovation and Product Development:
A competitive edge encourages innovation and ongoing product development. Companies that lack a clear differentiator may become complacent, hindering their ability to introduce new and improved products or services to meet changing customer needs.

Marketing Effectiveness:
Crafting compelling marketing messages becomes challenging without a unique selling proposition. Businesses must communicate what sets them apart to capture the attention of their target audience. A strong USP serves as the cornerstone for effective marketing campaigns.

Long-Term Sustainability:
A unique selling proposition contributes to the long-term sustainability of a business. Companies that continuously refine and reinforce their competitive edge are better positioned to withstand economic downturns, shifts in consumer behavior, and industry disruptions.

In a nutshell, the absence of a competitive edge or unique selling proposition leaves businesses susceptible to failure in an intensely competitive landscape. Establishing and nurturing a distinctive value proposition is not just a business strategy; it is a prerequisite for survival and prosperity in today's dynamic and ever-changing marketplace.

14

INEFFICIENT OPERATION AND PROCESSES

In the intricate dance of commerce, the efficiency of operations and processes is the heartbeat of a successful business. Companies that neglect the optimization of their workflows risk stumbling into a perilous path that leads to failure.

Increased Costs:

Inefficient operations often translate to higher costs. From redundant processes to unnecessary delays, every inefficiency contributes to an inflated operational budget. Businesses that fail to streamline their operations find themselves burdened with unnecessary expenses, impacting profitability.

Reduced Productivity:
Inefficiencies can throttle productivity, hampering the timely completion of tasks. Delays cascade through the organization, affecting overall output. A lack of streamlined processes stifles innovation and responsiveness, hindering the ability to meet customer demands and market changes promptly.

Customer Dissatisfaction:
In a world where customers expect seamless experiences, inefficient operations can result in delays, errors, and poor service. Unhappy customers are quick to seek alternatives, and negative experiences can tarnish a company's reputation, leading to loss of business and brand trust.

Missed Opportunities:
Business opportunities are often time-sensitive. Inefficient processes can lead to missed deadlines and delayed decision-making, causing a company to lose out on potential partnerships, collaborations, or market advantages. Agility is a key factor in seizing opportunities in a competitive landscape.

Employee Frustration and Turnover:
Workers tasked with navigating inefficient processes may experience frustration and burnout. High levels of dissatisfaction can lead to increased employee turnover, disrupting continuity, and costing the

business valuable talent. Efficient operations contribute to a positive work environment.

Lack of Scalability:
Inefficient processes struggle to scale with the growth of a business. As operations become more complex, outdated systems may buckle under the pressure, hindering expansion. Scalability is essential for long-term success, and inefficient operations can act as a roadblock to growth.

Compliance and Quality Issues:
In regulated industries, inefficiencies can lead to compliance lapses. Failure to adhere to industry standards and quality control measures can result in legal troubles, damaged relationships with stakeholders, and tarnished brand reputation.

Technology Integration Challenges:
Failure to embrace technology and automate processes can perpetuate inefficiencies. Companies that resist adopting innovative tools may find themselves at a technological disadvantage, struggling to keep up with competitors who leverage the latest advancements.

The impact of inefficient operations on a business cannot be overstated. It goes beyond mere inconvenience; it is a silent saboteur that erodes profits, damages reputations, and jeopardizes the very existence of a company. Smart businesses recognize the importance of continuous improvement, investing time and resources to ensure that their operations are not just functional but optimized for sustained success.

15

<u>POOR TIME MANAGEMENT</u>

Time, the most valuable and finite resource, can be either a business's greatest asset or its Achilles' heel. Poor time management is not just a personal shortcoming; it is a silent underminer that can lead a company down a path of inefficiency, missed opportunities, and ultimately, failure.

Missed Deadlines and Lost Opportunities:
Poor time management often results in missed deadlines. Whether it's delivering products, meeting client expectations, or responding to market trends, failure to manage time effectively can cause businesses to miss crucial opportunities, hindering growth and profitability.

Reduced Productivity and Output:
Businesses thrive on productivity. Poor time management leads to a fragmented work environment where tasks take longer to complete, and output diminishes. The cumulative effect can be a significant blow to a company's ability to meet demand and remain competitive.

Increased Stress and Burnout:
An organization plagued by poor time management is an organization under constant stress. Employees may find themselves overwhelmed, leading to burnout and a decrease in overall morale. A stressed workforce is less creative, less engaged, and more likely to make mistakes.

Ineffective Decision-Making:
Time is a critical factor in decision-making. Poor time management leaves businesses with insufficient time to gather relevant data,

analyze trends, and make informed decisions. Hasty decisions, made under time pressure, are often flawed and can have long-term consequences.

Customer Dissatisfaction:
In today's fast-paced world, customers expect prompt responses and timely deliveries. Poor time management can result in delayed communication, slow order fulfillment, and overall dissatisfaction. Unhappy customers are quick to seek alternatives, leading to a loss of revenue and a damaged reputation.

Resource Wastage:
Time is a resource, and poor management leads to its wastage. Whether it's excessive meetings, redundant processes, or delayed projects, businesses that do not value and optimize their time often squander valuable resources that could be better utilized elsewhere.

Hindered Innovation and Adaptability:
Innovation and adaptability are crucial for a business's survival. Poor time management stifles creativity and impedes the ability to adapt to market changes. Companies that cannot respond quickly to shifts in consumer preferences or industry trends risk becoming obsolete.

Erosion of Work-Life Balance:
Poor time management can blur the lines between work and personal life. Overworked and stressed employees are less likely to maintain a healthy work-life balance, leading to higher turnover rates and difficulties in attracting and retaining top talent.

Poor time management is not just a personal habit; it's a systemic issue that can have far-reaching consequences for a business. The failure to recognize and address this issue can result in a downward spiral of missed opportunities, dissatisfied customers, and stressed employees. Smart businesses prioritize effective time management as a cornerstone of their success, understanding that time, once lost, cannot be regained.

16
OVERRELIANCE ON A SINGLE CUSTOMER OR CLIENT

In the complicated dance of commerce, diversification is not just a strategic choice; it's a survival necessity. For businesses, placing all their eggs in one basket—relying heavily on a single customer or client—can create a precarious situation that leads to financial instability and, ultimately, failure.

Financial Vulnerability:
Depending on a single customer for the bulk of revenue exposes a business to financial vulnerability. If that customer decides to change suppliers, reduce orders, or face financial troubles themselves, the business reliant on them is left grappling with a sudden and significant loss of income.

Lack of Negotiating Power:
A business that relies too heavily on a single customer may find itself in a weakened negotiating position. When a significant portion of revenue comes from one source, the business has less leverage in negotiations, be it regarding pricing, payment terms, or other contractual agreements.

Market Fluctuations and Industry Changes:

Industries evolve, and market conditions change. Overreliance on a single customer can leave a business vulnerable to shifts in the market or changes in industry dynamics. Diversification helps spread the risk and provides a buffer against unforeseen challenges.

Limited Growth Opportunities:
Businesses aiming for growth need to expand their customer base. Relying on a single customer inhibits growth potential, as the business becomes overly dependent on the needs and stability of that particular client. Diversification is essential for tapping into new markets and opportunities.

Customer-Specific Risks:
Every customer relationship carries inherent risks. If a business is heavily reliant on one customer, any issues affecting that customer—such as management changes, financial troubles, or internal restructuring—directly impact the business. Diversification helps mitigate customer-specific risks.

Innovation Stagnation:
Overreliance on a single customer may lead to complacency. The business might become less motivated to innovate and adapt, relying on the stability of its existing customers. This lack of proactive innovation can hinder the company's ability to stay competitive in a rapidly changing business environment.

Reduced Flexibility:
A diverse customer base provides flexibility in navigating economic uncertainties. Businesses dependent on a single customer are less equipped to weather downturns, economic recessions, or unforeseen disruptions. Diversification ensures that a company can pivot and adapt to changing circumstances.

Reputation Risk:
If a business relies heavily on one customer and that customer experiences negative publicity or a damaged reputation, the dependent business may also suffer. Diversification helps mitigate the risk of reputational damage by distributing the impact across a broader customer base.

Overreliance on a single customer is akin to building a business on shaky ground. Diversification is not just a strategy; it's a safeguard against the unpredictable nature of the business landscape. Companies that recognize the dangers of putting all their eggs in one basket are better equipped to build a resilient and sustainable foundation for long-term success.

17

INEFFECTIVE COST CONTROL AND EXPENSE MANAGEMENT

In the sophisticated prom of business, financial prudence is not just a best practice; it's a survival imperative. For businesses, the inability to effectively control costs and manage expenses can create a perilous situation that leads to financial instability and, ultimately, failure.

Eroded Profit Margins:
Ineffective cost control allows expenses to balloon, eating into profit margins. Businesses that fail to manage costs find themselves struggling to maintain healthy financial returns, impacting their ability to invest in growth initiatives or weather economic uncertainties.

Cash Flow Challenges:
A business's cash flow is its lifeblood. Inadequate expense management can lead to cash flow challenges, making it difficult to cover operational costs, pay suppliers, or seize time-sensitive opportunities. A healthy cash flow is essential for sustaining day-to-day operations and fueling growth.

Reduced Competitiveness:
Inefficient cost structures make it challenging for a business to remain competitive. Competitors who excel at cost control can offer products or services at lower prices, potentially luring away customers and eroding market share. Effective cost management is a cornerstone of long-term competitiveness.

Increased Debt and Financial Strain:
Businesses grappling with ineffective cost control may resort to borrowing to cover ongoing expenses. Accumulating debt can create a cycle of financial strain, with interest payments further burdening the company's financial health. Over time, this can lead to insurmountable challenges.

Inhibited Investment in Innovation:
Cost control is not just about cutting expenses; it's about allocating resources wisely. Businesses that struggle with ineffective cost management may find it difficult to invest in research, development, and innovation. This inhibits their ability to stay ahead of market trends and customer expectations.

Employee Morale and Productivity:
Cost-cutting measures, if not managed effectively, can impact employee morale and productivity. Layoffs, reduced benefits, or cutbacks in training programs can lead to a disengaged workforce,

diminishing overall productivity and hindering the company's ability to achieve its goals.

Inability to Weather Economic Downturns:
Sound cost control is crucial for preparing a business to weather economic downturns. In times of recession or market volatility, companies with ineffective expense management are more vulnerable, lacking the financial reserves to navigate challenges and emerge stronger on the other side.

Stakeholder Confidence Erosion:
Investors, creditors, and other stakeholders closely monitor a company's financial health. Ineffective cost control erodes stakeholder confidence, leading to reduced investment, higher interest rates on loans, and a diminished ability to attract capital. Maintaining trust is essential for long-term business success.

The failure to effectively control costs is a silent threat that can undermine the very foundation of a business. It goes beyond balancing the books; it is a strategic imperative for sustained success. Companies that prioritize prudent expense management position themselves not only for financial stability but also for agility and resilience in an ever-evolving business landscape.

18
FAILURE TO DELEGATE OR TRUST EMPLOYEES

In sophisticated 20th-century business, effective leadership is not just about making decisions; it's about empowering a team to excel. For businesses, the failure to delegate tasks and trust employees can create a precarious situation that leads to stifled growth, decreased morale, and, ultimately, failure.

Bottlenecked Decision-Making:
A leader who fails to delegate often becomes a bottleneck in the decision-making process. This hampers the company's ability to respond quickly to opportunities or challenges, hindering innovation and adaptability in a fast-paced business environment.

Employee Stagnation:
An unwillingness to delegate can stunt employee growth and development. When employees are not given the chance to take on new responsibilities and challenges, their skills and potential remain untapped. This lack of professional growth can lead to dissatisfaction and disengagement.

Limited Strategic Vision:
Effective delegation is essential for strategic planning and vision implementation. Leaders who try to manage every detail find it challenging to focus on the bigger picture. A lack of strategic vision can result in a business that operates reactively rather than proactively.

Decreased Employee Morale:
A failure to trust employees can erode morale. When team members feel micromanaged or that their capabilities are not recognized, it leads to frustration and demotivation. A disheartened workforce is less likely to be innovative, collaborative, and committed to achieving the company's goals.

Hindered Creativity and Innovation:

Innovation thrives in an environment where employees feel empowered to contribute their ideas. Leaders who resist delegation may inadvertently stifle creativity by limiting the diversity of perspectives and ideas brought to the table. This can hinder a company's ability to stay ahead in a competitive market.

Time Mismanagement:
Leaders who struggle to delegate often find themselves overwhelmed with tasks that could be handled by capable team members. This mismanagement of time prevents leaders from focusing on high-impact activities, hindering their effectiveness in guiding the company toward success.

Employee Burnout:
A failure to delegate can lead to overworked and burnt-out employees. When individuals are consistently tasked with more than they can handle, it not only affects their well-being but also decreases overall productivity and increases the risk of turnover.

Lack of Succession Planning:
Effective delegation is integral to succession planning. Leaders who fail to delegate may neglect to groom the next generation of leaders within the organization. This lack of preparation can lead to a leadership vacuum in times of transition or unexpected departures.

In a nutshell, the inability to delegate is not just a leadership flaw; it's a business risk that can have far-reaching consequences. Companies that recognize the value of empowering their teams, fostering trust, and embracing delegation build a foundation for sustainable success. Delegation is not a sign of weakness; it's a strategic choice that enables businesses to tap into the collective talents and potential of their workforce.

19

IGNORING THE IMPORTANCE OF NETWORKING AND RELATIONSHIP

In the ever-dynamic world of business, success is not solely measured by-products and profits; it is equally reliant on relationships and networks. For businesses, ignoring the importance of networking can create a perilous situation that leads to missed opportunities, diminished brand influence, and, ultimately, failure.

Limited Business Opportunities:
Networking is the gateway to a myriad of business opportunities. Ignoring the power of connections and relationships means missing out on potential collaborations, partnerships, and valuable insights. Businesses that operate in isolation limit their ability to tap into a broader ecosystem of possibilities.

Impaired Reputation and Trust:
Networking is a cornerstone of building a positive reputation in the business community. Ignoring relationship-building efforts can result in a lack of trust and credibility. In an era where reputation is a currency, a damaged business image can deter potential clients, partners, and investors.

Hindered Market Awareness:
Networking is a vital channel for spreading awareness about a business and its offerings. Without active engagement in relevant networks, a company may struggle to make its presence known. This lack of visibility can lead to decreased market share and lost growth opportunities.

Missed Industry Trends and Insights:
Networking provides a platform for staying informed about industry trends, market shifts, and emerging opportunities. A business that ignores these connections risks falling behind, unaware of changes that could impact its strategy and competitiveness.

Limited Access to Talent:
Talent acquisition is a critical aspect of business success. Ignoring networking means limited access to potential employees, industry experts, and key influencers. A robust network opens doors to a pool of skilled professionals, enhancing the company's ability to attract top talent.

Ineffective Marketing Strategies:
Networking is intertwined with effective marketing. Businesses that operate in isolation miss the chance to leverage word-of-mouth referrals, endorsements, and collaborative marketing efforts. A lack of networking can result in less impactful marketing strategies and reduced customer acquisition.

Slower Innovation and Adaptation:
Networking facilitates the exchange of ideas and insights. Ignoring this aspect can lead to a lack of exposure to innovative concepts and industry best practices. A business that operates in a silo may struggle to adapt to changing market conditions and evolving customer expectations.

Lack of Emotional Capital:
Building relationships is not just transactional; it's about creating emotional capital. Ignoring networking means overlooking the human element in business. Emotional connections with clients, partners, and

stakeholders can be a powerful differentiator, fostering loyalty and long-term collaboration.

The failure to recognize the importance of networking is akin to navigating uncharted waters without a compass. Businesses that invest in relationships, actively participate in networks and prioritize building a robust professional community position themselves for sustained success. Networking is not a mere formality; it is a strategic imperative that fuels growth, innovation, and resilience in an ever-evolving business landscape.

20
INADEQUATE CONTINGENCY PLANNING FOR EMERGENCIES

In the unpredictable realm of business, the ability to weather storms and emerge stronger is a hallmark of resilience. For businesses, the failure to establish comprehensive contingency plans for emergencies can create a vulnerable situation that leads to operational chaos, reputational damage, and, ultimately, failure.

Operational Disruption:
Emergencies, whether natural disasters, cybersecurity breaches, or unexpected market shifts, have the potential to disrupt normal business operations. Without adequate contingency planning, a company may find itself paralyzed, unable to respond effectively to the challenges posed by unforeseen events.

Financial Strain:
Inadequate contingency planning often translates to financial strain. Emergencies may require significant financial resources for recovery

efforts, legal liabilities, and potential losses. A business unprepared for such scenarios can face insurmountable financial challenges, jeopardizing its very existence.

Damage to Reputation:
A lack of preparedness in the face of emergencies can lead to a tarnished reputation. Stakeholders, including customers, investors, and partners, closely monitor how a business handles crises. Inadequate contingency planning may result in poor crisis management, damaging trust and credibility.

Loss of Critical Data:
Cybersecurity threats are a constant concern in the digital age. Inadequate contingency planning for data breaches or system failures puts a business at risk of losing critical information. The aftermath of such incidents can include legal consequences, regulatory penalties, and long-term damage to the company's data integrity.

Employee Morale and Productivity:
Emergencies can take a toll on employee morale and productivity. Without a clear plan in place, employees may feel uncertain about their roles and the future of the company. This uncertainty can lead to decreased productivity, increased stress, and higher turnover rates.

Supply Chain Disruptions:
Contingency planning is essential for businesses reliant on supply chains. Emergencies such as natural disasters or geopolitical events can disrupt the flow of goods and services. Companies without contingency plans for supply chain interruptions risk being unable to meet customer demand and facing increased costs.

Regulatory Compliance Issues:

In some industries, emergencies may trigger regulatory scrutiny and compliance requirements. Inadequate contingency planning can result in non-compliance, leading to legal consequences, fines, and a damaged relationship with regulatory bodies.

Inability to Seize Opportunities:
Effective contingency planning is not only about mitigating risks but also about seizing opportunities in the face of adversity. Businesses with inadequate plans may miss the chance to pivot, innovate, or gain a competitive advantage during challenging times.

The failure to establish comprehensive contingency plans is akin to sailing without a lifeboat in stormy seas. Businesses that prioritize preparedness, proactive risk assessment, and effective crisis management position themselves not just for survival but for resilience and sustained success. Contingency planning is not a luxury; it is a strategic imperative that ensures a business can navigate unforeseen challenges and emerge stronger on the other side.

21

IGNORING THE COMPETITION

In the dynamic landscape of the business world, the strategy of ignoring competition might seem like a tempting approach for some entrepreneurs. However, this seemingly blissful ignorance can quickly turn into a recipe for failure. Here's why keeping a close eye on competitors is crucial for sustainable success:

Market Trends and Innovation:

Ignoring competitors means overlooking evolving market trends and innovations. Businesses that fail to adapt risk becoming outdated and unable to meet the changing needs of their customers. By monitoring the competition, companies can stay abreast of industry advancements and maintain a competitive edge.

Customer Insights:
Competitors often provide valuable insights into customer preferences and behavior. Dismissing this information can fail to understand the evolving demands of the target audience. Acknowledging and leveraging competitor data can help businesses tailor their products or services to better meet customer expectations.

Benchmarking Performance:
Ignoring competition means missing out on valuable benchmarking opportunities. Regularly assessing how a business compares to its competitors in terms of performance, pricing, and customer satisfaction allows for strategic adjustments. Without benchmarking, a company may inadvertently fall behind in crucial areas.

Price Wars and Differentiation:
Failing to acknowledge the pricing strategies of competitors can lead to unintended price wars or undervaluing products. Understanding the pricing landscape helps businesses position themselves effectively, emphasizing unique value propositions to stand out in the market.

Strategic Alliances and Partnerships:
Ignorance of the competitive landscape may result in missed opportunities for strategic alliances or partnerships. Collaborations with other businesses can open new avenues for growth, enhance capabilities, and strengthen market positioning. Awareness of competitors facilitates the identification of potential collaborators.

Marketing and Branding Insights:
Analyzing competitor marketing and branding strategies can provide valuable insights into what resonates with the target audience. Businesses that disregard this information risk creating messages that fail to connect with customers or miss opportunities to differentiate themselves effectively.

Risk Mitigation:
Ignoring the competitive landscape can blindside a business to potential risks. Changes in competitor strategies, economic shifts, or industry disruptions may catch a business off guard. Staying informed allows for proactive risk mitigation and strategic planning to navigate challenges effectively.

While focusing on one's strengths is essential, turning a blind eye to the competition can be a costly mistake. Business success requires a balanced approach that combines self-awareness with a keen understanding of the competitive landscape. By learning from competitors and adapting strategies accordingly, businesses can position themselves for sustained growth and resilience in a rapidly changing market.

22

LACK OF PERSEVERANCE AND RESILIENCE

In the tumultuous journey of entrepreneurship, the virtues of perseverance and resilience emerge as indispensable pillars for sustained success. Failing to cultivate and embody these qualities can significantly increase the risk of business failure. Here's a closer look at how the absence of perseverance and resilience can prove detrimental:

Navigating Challenges:
Business landscapes are fraught with challenges, from economic downturns to unexpected crises. Lack of perseverance may lead entrepreneurs to abandon ship at the first sign of trouble. Resilience, on the other hand, empowers businesses to weather storms, learn from setbacks, and emerge stronger on the other side.

Adaptability to Change:
Markets are dynamic, and adaptability is key to survival. Without perseverance, businesses may struggle to implement necessary changes and adapt to evolving circumstances. Resilience ensures that setbacks are viewed as opportunities to learn and pivot, fostering a culture of continuous improvement.

Long-Term Vision:
Business success often requires a long-term perspective. A lack of perseverance can result in a shortsighted approach, where entrepreneurs focus on immediate gains rather than enduring success. Resilience, however, allows businesses to stay committed to their vision, even when faced with short-term challenges.

Learning from Failure:
Every business encounters failures, but it is the ability to bounce back that distinguishes successful ventures. Perseverance fuels the drive to learn from mistakes, while resilience enables businesses to turn setbacks into valuable lessons, paving the way for future growth and innovation.

Building Trust and Credibility:
Consistency is fundamental to building trust and credibility in the business world. Lack of perseverance can erode trust, as stakeholders may question the commitment of the business to its goals. Resilience, however, fosters trust by demonstrating an unwavering dedication to overcoming obstacles.

Employee Morale and Productivity:
The attitude of business leaders sets the tone for the entire organization. A lack of perseverance can create a negative atmosphere, impacting employee morale and productivity. Resilience, on the other hand, inspires a sense of purpose and determination among the team, driving them to overcome challenges collectively.

Entrepreneurial Mindset:
Perseverance and resilience are foundational elements of the entrepreneurial mindset. Entrepreneurs who lack these qualities may struggle to sustain the passion and drive needed to navigate the highs and lows of business ownership. Resilience ensures that setbacks are viewed as part of the entrepreneurial journey rather than insurmountable obstacles.

Market Competition:
The business landscape is highly competitive, requiring tenacity to stand out. Lack of perseverance can result in businesses giving up on differentiation efforts, leading to mediocrity. Resilience empowers businesses to persist in their pursuit of excellence, making them more competitive in the long run.

The journey of entrepreneurship is not for the faint of heart. Perseverance and resilience serve as the bedrock upon which successful businesses are built. Embracing these qualities enables entrepreneurs to navigate challenges, adapt to change, and ultimately thrive in a dynamic and unpredictable business environment. As businesses face inevitable hurdles, it is the unwavering commitment to persevere and the resilience to bounce back that pave the way for enduring success.

23

POOR WORK-LIFE BALANCE

In the fast-paced world of business, achieving a healthy work-life balance is often overshadowed by the demands of entrepreneurship. However, neglecting this equilibrium can have profound consequences, potentially leading to failure in the business realm. Here's a closer examination of how poor work-life balance can adversely affect businesses:

Burnout and Reduced Productivity:
An imbalanced work-life dynamic can contribute to burnout among employees and business leaders alike. Burnout diminishes productivity, creativity, and overall job satisfaction. A workforce burdened by excessive work hours may experience diminishing returns, hindering the efficiency and effectiveness of business operations.

Employee Retention and Recruitment Challenges:
Businesses that consistently prioritize work over the well-being of their employees may struggle to retain top talent and attract new skilled professionals. A poor work-life balance can lead to high turnover rates, creating instability within the organization and impeding the building of a cohesive and skilled team.

Creativity and Innovation Stagnation:
Continuous work without adequate breaks can stifle creativity and innovation. A lack of time for relaxation and rejuvenation inhibits the mind's ability to think creatively. Businesses that neglect work-life balance risk becoming stagnant, unable to adapt to market changes or introduce innovative solutions.

Health Issues Impacting Performance:
Poor work-life balance can contribute to physical and mental health issues among employees. Chronic stress, fatigue, and a sedentary lifestyle can result in health-related challenges that affect job performance. Unhealthy employees are less likely to perform optimally, impacting the overall health of the business.

Strained Professional and Personal Relationships:
Overemphasis on work at the expense of personal life can strain relationships. This strain can extend to professional interactions within the business, affecting collaboration and teamwork. A harmonious work environment, fostered by a healthy work-life balance, is crucial for the success of any business.

Ineffective Decision-Making:
Exhaustion and stress resulting from poor work-life balance can impair decision-making abilities. Critical business decisions require a clear and focused mind. When leaders are fatigued or overwhelmed, the quality of decision-making diminishes, potentially leading to misguided strategies and poor outcomes.

Reputation and Brand Perception:
Businesses that are perceived as neglectful of their employees' well-being may suffer damage to their reputation and brand image. In an

era where corporate social responsibility is increasingly valued, a lack of concern for work-life balance can be detrimental to a company's public perception.

Lack of Adaptability to Change:
Rapid changes in the business environment demand agility and adaptability. A workforce burdened by poor work-life balance may lack the resilience needed to navigate change effectively. Businesses that are unable to adapt risk falling behind in the face of evolving market dynamics.

The repercussions of poor work-life balance extend beyond the individual to impact the very fabric of a business. Striking the right balance between professional responsibilities and personal well-being is not just a matter of employee satisfaction but a crucial element in fostering a resilient, innovative, and successful business. Recognizing and prioritizing work-life balance is an investment in the long-term health and prosperity of both employees and the business as a whole.

24
NOT INVESTING IN SELF-IMPROVEMENT AND LEARNING

In the fast-paced and competitive landscape of business, the importance of continuous self-improvement and learning cannot be overstated. Failing to invest time and resources in personal development can have dire consequences for entrepreneurs and business professionals alike. Let's explore how neglecting self-improvement can become a stumbling block on the path to success.

Stagnation in Skills:
In a dynamic business environment, staying relevant is crucial. Failing to invest in acquiring new skills or updating existing ones can result in a stagnant skill set. As industries evolve and technologies advance, those who don't adapt may find themselves unable to meet the demands of their market.

Lack of Innovation:
Business success often hinges on innovation. Without a commitment to self-improvement, individuals may struggle to think creatively and come up with fresh ideas. Innovation is the lifeblood of business, and a failure to foster it can lead to a loss of competitive edge.

Ineffective Leadership:
Leadership is not a static quality; it requires continuous refinement. Those who neglect personal growth may find themselves ill-equipped to lead effectively. Leadership skills, emotional intelligence, and adaptability are all aspects that demand ongoing attention and development.

Poor Decision-Making:
In the absence of continuous learning, decision-making abilities may suffer. Business landscapes are riddled with complexities, and without a commitment to learning, individuals may struggle to make informed and strategic decisions, increasing the risk of failure.

Missed Opportunities:
Opportunities often arise from staying informed and being prepared. A lack of investment in self-improvement may result in individuals being oblivious to potential opportunities or being unprepared to seize them. This can hinder both personal and business growth.

Burnout and Stress:
Neglecting personal well-being can lead to burnout and chronic stress, negatively impacting one's ability to perform at their best. A healthy work-life balance and stress management are integral components of sustained business success.

Diminished Adaptability:
Business landscapes are subject to rapid changes. Those who resist learning and self-improvement risk becoming obsolete. Adaptability is a key trait for success, and failure to cultivate it can leave individuals and businesses vulnerable in the face of change.

In a nutshell, the journey to success in business is intertwined with a commitment to self-improvement and continuous learning. Failing to make this investment can result in a myriad of challenges, from a stagnant skill set to missed opportunities and diminished adaptability. To thrive in today's business world, individuals must recognize the value of ongoing personal development as an integral part of the path to success.

25

SUCCUMBING TO FEAR OF FAILURE OR TAKING EXCESSIVE RISKS

In the intricate dance of entrepreneurship, finding the delicate equilibrium between a healthy respect for failure and calculated risk-taking is paramount. Succumbing to the fear of failure or, conversely, embracing excessive risks can both lead down a perilous path toward business failure. Let's delve into the consequences of these extremes and explore the art of balancing fear and risk.

Paralysis by Fear:
The fear of failure, while a natural human instinct, can paralyze decision-making and hinder progress. Entrepreneurs who allow fear to dictate their actions may avoid necessary risks, stifling innovation and growth. This fear-driven paralysis can lead to missed opportunities and stagnant business development.

Missed Innovation Opportunities:
Innovation often involves an element of risk. Those who succumb to the fear of failure may shy away from groundbreaking ideas or unconventional approaches. Consequently, their businesses may lag behind competitors who embrace calculated risks to push the boundaries of innovation.

Excessive Risk-Taking:
On the flip side, an overzealous pursuit of risk can be equally detrimental. Entrepreneurs enticed by the allure of high-risk, high-reward scenarios may expose their businesses to unnecessary vulnerabilities. Unbridled risk-taking can lead to financial instability, reputational damage, and, ultimately, business failure.

Financial Instability:
Taking excessive risks without a solid foundation can jeopardize financial stability. Businesses may find themselves overleveraged or invested in ventures with insufficient market research. Financial mismanagement resulting from unchecked risk-taking can lead to insurmountable challenges.

Lack of Strategic Planning:
Success in business often involves strategic planning and thoughtful decision-making. Succumbing to the fear of failure or indulging in

excessive risks may disrupt the delicate balance required for effective strategic planning. Businesses may operate reactively rather than proactively, increasing the likelihood of failure.

Strained Team Dynamics:
The emotional toll of fear or excessive risk-taking can strain team dynamics. Fear-driven leaders may create a culture of caution and micromanagement, stifling creativity. Conversely, excessive risk-takers may foster an environment of instability and anxiety among team members.

Reputational Damage:
Both fear-driven conservatism and reckless risk-taking can harm a business's reputation. Customers, investors, and partners seek reliability and stability. A business that swings between extremes may struggle to maintain a positive public image, potentially leading to loss of trust.

The journey of entrepreneurship requires a delicate balance between acknowledging the fear of failure and embracing calculated risks. Succumbing entirely to fear can lead to stagnation, while excessive risk-taking may result in instability and failure. Successful business leaders navigate this thin line with resilience, prudence, and a keen understanding of when to hold back and when to leap forward. Achieving this balance is an art that separates thriving businesses from those that succumb to the extremes of fear or recklessness.